OUT OF THIS WORLD

Meet NASA Inventor Lynn Rothschild and Her Team's

Martian Fungoid Space Base

WORLD BOOK

www.worldbook.com

World Book, Inc.
180 North LaSalle Street
Suite 900
Chicago, Illinois 60601
USA

For information about other World Book publications, visit our website at www.worldbook.com or call 1-800-WORLDBK (967-5325).

For information about sales to schools and libraries, call 1-800-975-3250 (United States), or 1-800-837-5365 (Canada).

© 2024 (print and e-book) by World Book, Inc. All rights reserved. No part of this publication may be reproduced, stored in a retrieval system, or transmitted in any form or by any means (electronic, mechanical, photocopying, recording, or otherwise) without written permission from World Book, Inc.

WORLD BOOK and the GLOBE DEVICE are registered trademarks or trademarks of World Book, Inc.

Produced in collaboration with the National Aeronautics and Space Administration (NASA).

Library of Congress Cataloging-in-Publication Data for this volume has been applied for.

Out of This World
ISBN: 978-0-7166-6564-9 (set, hc.)

Martian Fungoid Space Base
ISBN: 978-0-7166-6570-0 (hc.)

Also available as:
ISBN: 978-0-7166-6578-6 (e-book)
ISBN: 978-0-7166-6586-1 (soft cover)

Staff

Editorial

Vice President
Tom Evans

Senior Manager, New Content
Jeff De La Rosa

Writer
William D. Adams

Editor
Emma Flickinger

Curriculum Designer
Caroline Davidson

Proofreader
Nathalie Strassheim

Indexer
Nathaniel Lindstrom

Graphics and Design

Senior Visual
Communications Designer
Melanie Bender

Digital Asset Specialist
Rosalia Bledsoe

Acknowledgments

Cover	redhouse studio	22-23	University of Massachusetts Amherst
3	redhouse studio; © Kallayanee Naloka, Shutterstock	24-25	2018 Stanford-Brown-RISD iGEM Team; © MycoBond
4-5	© Elena11/Shutterstock	26-27	redhouse studio
6-7	© Photon75/Shutterstock	29	Lynn Rothschild
8-9	© Platoo Studio/Shutterstock	30-31	© Alexlky/Shutterstock; redhouse studio
10-11	Juan de Vojníkov (licensed under CC BY-SA 4.0 DEED); © Peter Hermes Furian, Shutterstock; Picturepest (licensed under CC BY 2.0 DEED)	32-33	redhouse studio
		34-35	Lynn Rothschild
		37	Cambridge University Library
12-13	NASA	38-39	NASA
14-15	Lynn Rothschild	40-41	© Juergen Faelchle, Shutterstock
16-17	redhouse studio	42-43	NASA
18-19	© ASCHW/Shutterstock	44	Lynn Rothschild
20-21	© Kallayanee Naloka, Shutterstock; © Karel Bock, Shutterstock		

Contents

- **4** Introduction
- **6** The way of the turtle
- **8** The way of the bird
- **10** INVENTOR FEATURE: Hands-on learning
- **12** BIG IDEA: The moon as proving ground for Mars
- **14** INVENTOR FEATURE: From scientist to engineer-scientist
- **16** BIG IDEA: Life as a technology
- **18** What is a fungus?
- **22** INVENTOR FEATURE: Mentors
- **24** Mycelium composite materials
- **26** BIG IDEA: Inflatable-form mycotecture
- **28** INVENTOR FEATURE: Hobbies and field trips
- **30** Feeding the fungi
- **32** Baking the form
- **34** Prototypes
- **36** INVENTOR FEATURE: Darwin
- **38** Planetary protection
- **42** Experiments
- **44** Lynn's team
- **45** Glossary
- **46** Review and reflect
- **48** Index

Glossary There is a glossary of terms on page 45. Terms defined in the glossary are in boldface type that **looks like this** on their first appearance on any spread (two facing pages).

Pronunciations (how to say words) are given in parentheses the first time some difficult words appear in the book. They look like this: pronunciation (pruh NUHN see AY shuhn).

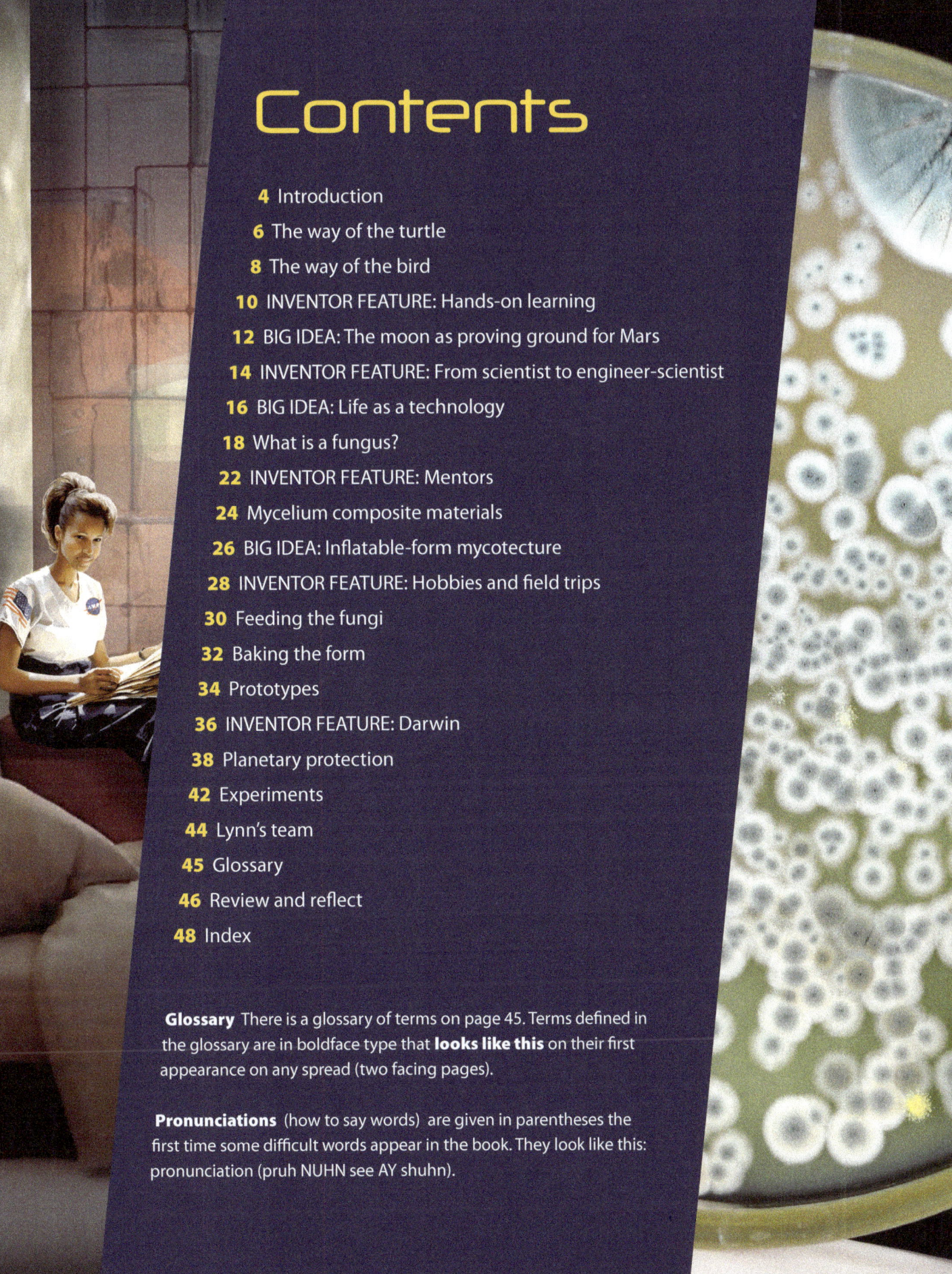

Introduction

Humans want to explore—and eventually colonize—other worlds. This is the greatest technological challenge of all time. The basic protections we take for granted on Earth are mostly or totally absent on other worlds. Earth's thick **atmosphere** holds life-giving oxygen, moderates temperatures, shields the planet from dangerous space debris, and protects life from harmful **radiation.**

How do you re-create such protections to provide astronauts and colonists with safe, healthy, and comfortable lives? Lynn Rothschild, a biologist at NASA's Ames Research Center, wants to use life itself as the technology to enable humans to survive and thrive off-planet. She and her team are exploring the use of such living things as fungus as a building material. Such materials could be used to create safe, comfortable structures on the moon and Mars.

The NASA Innovative Advanced Concepts program. The titles in the *Out of This World* series feature projects that have won grant money from a group formed by the United States National Aeronautics and Space Administration, or NASA. The NASA Innovative Advanced Concepts program (NIAC) provides funding to teams working to develop bold new advances in space technology. You can visit NIAC's website at www.nasa.gov/niac.

Meet Lynn Rothschild.

" Since I was child, I've been interested in microscopic living things and how they thrive in diverse and extreme conditions. Now, I'm finding ways to put these **microbes** to work for astronauts exploring other worlds. "

The way of the turtle

Lynn compares conventional plans for housing astronauts to the way a turtle carries its shell.

❝ A turtle always has its **habitat** with it. ❞ —Lynn

Likewise, astronauts have traditionally carried their shelter in the form of a spacecraft. This approach is reliable. Astronauts are guaranteed to have a functional habitat when they arrive at their destination.

Any Mars mission is going to take time because of its great distance from Earth. But, with a conventional approach, this time is compounded by the need for preparation missions. Missions containing habitation modules, robotic construction **probes,** and supplies would be launched long before the first crews could even arrive. Preparing the base would take years. Furthermore, such a base would need a constant stream of supplies from Earth. Therefore, a turtle-based mission approach would be extremely expensive and difficult to maintain.

Stranded on Mars

It takes about six months to reach Mars. But even this seemingly long trip is only possible for a window every two years, when the **orbits** of Earth and Mars align for minimum travel time. At other times, astronauts would be stranded on Mars—even if they had a return craft. All the more reason for Mars missions to be as self-sustaining as possible!

The way of the bird

To get to Mars, Lynn suggests that we should build structures more in the way that a bird builds a nest.

❚❚ A bird is able to look at what the conditions are and design and build specifically for that location. ❚❚ —Lynn

A bird builds its nest out of the materials available in its environment. It can move much faster without having to carry its nest with it everywhere. A single bird can fly thousands of miles or kilometers per year, nesting in one location and finding food in another.

A birdlike approach will require Martian astronauts and colonists to be much more self-sufficient. They will have to build their own shelter, grow their own food, produce their own air, and provide their own water. More importantly, they will have to be prepared for any problems that might occur. If something breaks, astronauts need to be able to fix it. If an astronaut gets injured or sick, other astronauts will have to provide medical care.

Birds, such as this weaver bird, construct their nest with materials they have on hand.

Inventor feature:
Hands-on learning

Lynn's journey into science began when she looked through the lenses of a microscope.

❚❚ We used a microscope for three days when I was in third grade. The first day, we looked at a human hair. The second day, we looked at an onion cell. The third day, we looked at an ameba, and I was absolutely hooked. ❚❚ —Lynn

Amebas are a group of one-celled living things. Some amebas live in water and moist soil. Others live in the bodies of animals and human beings.

Lynn begged her father for a microscope and then for identification keys for **microbes.**

❚❚ Kids have hobbies. One of my hobbies was raising protozoa! ❚❚ —Lynn

Lynn credits her inspiration to the value of looking at things yourself. For 10 years, she taught **astrobiology** and space exploration at Stanford University. Her students would barely react when she showed them fantastic pictures taken by the Hubble Space Telescope. But then, they would go on a field trip to a local observatory and use some modestly sized telescopes to look at the stars and planets.

> That was much more fascinating to these college students than the best images I could show them. I still think there's something really important about experiencing these things yourself. —Lynn

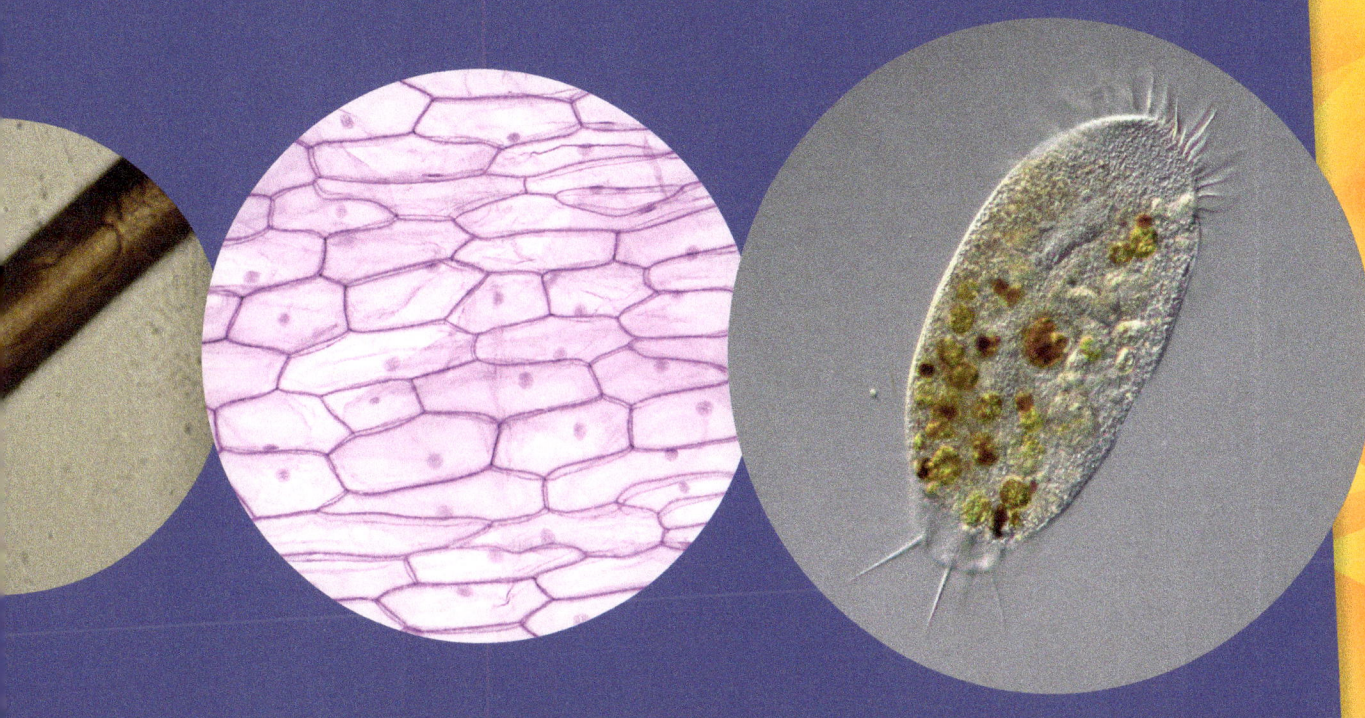

Big idea:
The moon as a proving ground for Mars

Crewed missions to Mars are still likely decades away. In the meantime, many countries are planning to develop a long-term presence on the moon.

The return to the moon will likely begin with a turtle-type mission structure. The moon is only a three-day journey from Earth. It will be easier to ship in supplies, send replacement parts, or evacuate astronauts if something goes wrong. Nevertheless, the moon will be a proving ground for a bird-style mission approach.

Space programs are targeting parts of the moon that could harbor water ice. Such ice will provide the opportunity to test harvesting resources in space. This technique is called *in situ resource utilization* (ISRU). *In situ* means *on-site*.

Water is heavy and therefore difficult to launch from Earth in great quantities. Astronauts or robotic machinery will mine the water ice out of lunar rocks. It can be used to make rocket fuel and oxygen as well as for drinking and for watering crops. If astronauts can successfully harvest water ice from the moon and convert it into useful products, their reliance on launches from Earth will decrease drastically.

Learning ISRU on the moon will help **engineers** and mission planners prepare for Mars. Lynn thinks that other flexible technologies could be demonstrated on the moon as well.

Artist's impression of a resource prospector on the lunar surface

Inventor feature:
From scientist to engineer-scientist

Lynn came to NASA as a scientist, to study **astrobiology.** Astrobiology is the search for other life in the universe. But she was "forced" to think about life in a different way:

> About 15 years ago or so, our center director at the time had this idea that biology would be helpful for technology for NASA. In fact, it could be the enabling technology for moving humans off the planet. He directed me to start a program around it. So that's why I was sort of forced into thinking about biology as technology. But when I say 'forced,' it was a good thing, because it turns out I had an aptitude for it and really enjoyed it. —Lynn

The shift in priority gave Lynn an appreciation for the difference between a scientist and an **engineer.**

> A scientist looks at the world the way it is…and tries to understand that. An engineer makes something new. —Lynn

But, the change also led to the realization that she could be both.

❞ It turns out that it's kind of fun making new things! I was asked to try to make something new—to be an engineer—using my biology background. ❞ —Lynn

Big idea:
Life as a technology

The exploration and colonization of other worlds is fraught with extremely difficult technological challenges. Living things have been overcoming environmental challenges for billions of years. Why not use them as a technology to help us overcome environmental problems on other worlds?

Other life technologies

Lynn is committed to the idea of using life as technology to achieve goals in space. She has other NIAC proposals for systems in which **microbes** could manufacture medicines for astronauts—and even recycle metals!

Lynn's idea is to build structures out of fungus on the moon and Mars. She envisions lightweight, safe, easy-to-assemble structures that could be quickly tailored to local conditions. But, how can people live within fungi?

What is a fungus?

Fungi are living things that obtain food by absorbing it from other living organisms or from parts of formerly living things. They are neither plants nor animals, having diverged from both over a billion years ago. Some fungi consist of only a single cell. Others make up some of the largest living things in the world.

Mushrooms are the fruiting bodies of many fungi, much like flowers are the fruiting bodies of many plants. Gills or tubes on the undersides of the mushrooms release *spores* (reproductive cells) into the environment.

Fungi are incredibly important to **ecosystems.** They *decompose* (break down) dead animal and plant matter and return the nutrients to the soil.

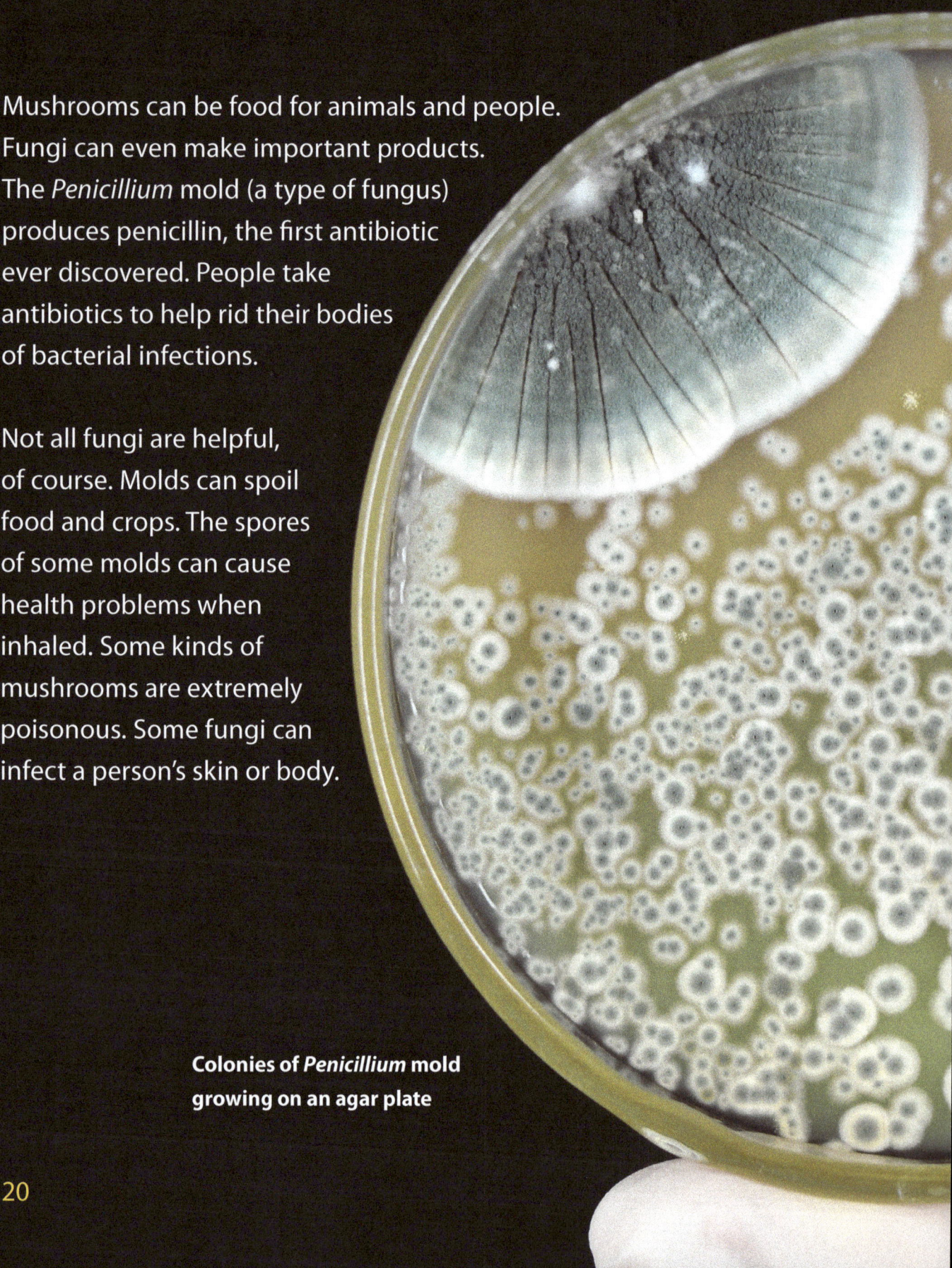

Mushrooms can be food for animals and people. Fungi can even make important products. The *Penicillium* mold (a type of fungus) produces penicillin, the first antibiotic ever discovered. People take antibiotics to help rid their bodies of bacterial infections.

Not all fungi are helpful, of course. Molds can spoil food and crops. The spores of some molds can cause health problems when inhaled. Some kinds of mushrooms are extremely poisonous. Some fungi can infect a person's skin or body.

Colonies of *Penicillium* mold growing on an agar plate

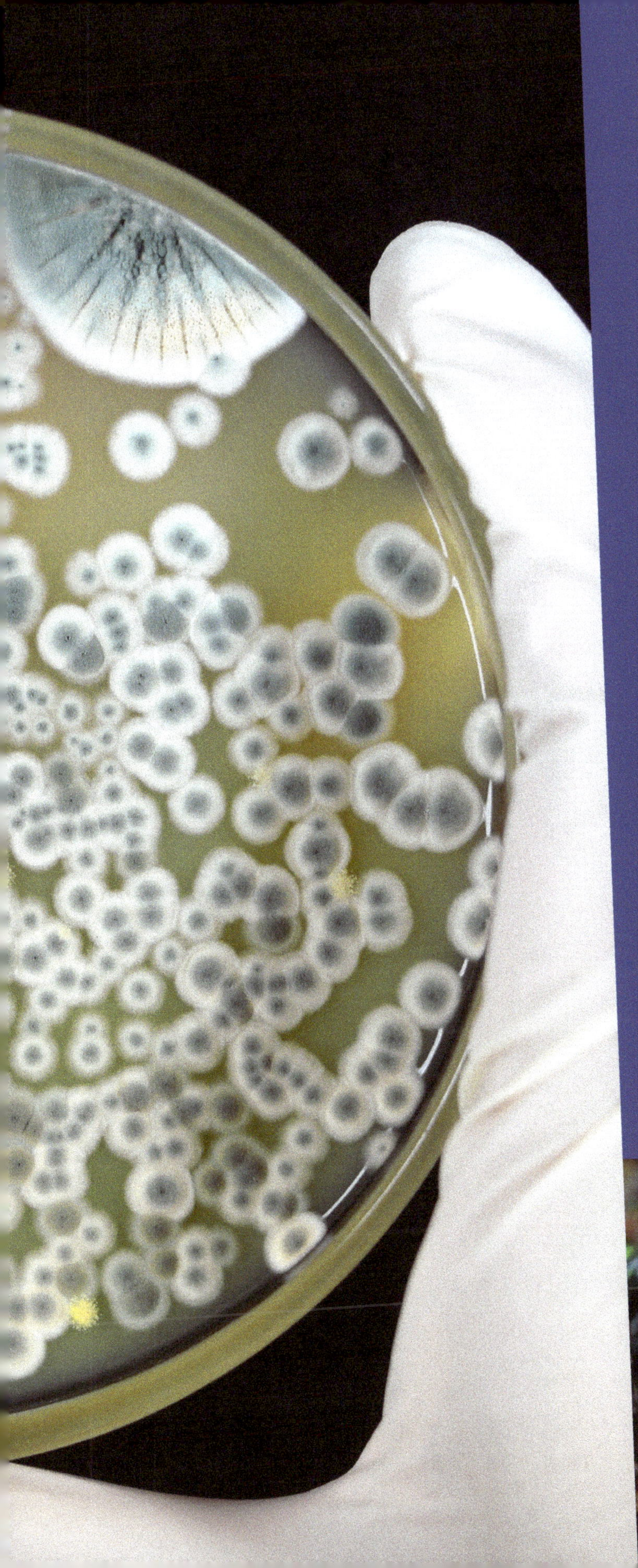

Humongous Fungus

Armillaria ostoyae is a kind of fungus that lives off trees in the Pacific Northwest region of the United States. *A. ostoyae* saps nutrients from a living fir tree, eventually killing it. After the tree dies, the fungus continues to feed on the decomposing trunk. This fungus spreads from tree to tree through special underground structures called *rhizomorphs*. The rhizomorphs enable a single individual to cover a large area. The largest-known *A. ostoyae* covers 2,385 acres (965 hectares) and is one of the largest organisms on Earth. Scientists have nicknamed it "the Humongous Fungus."

Inventor feature:
Mentors

❝ I did have some really great mentors, and that made all the difference. ❞ —Lynn

Lynn's support started with her family. Her father studied physics at Yale University and supported her interest in science. Both of Lynn's grandfathers supported her as well.

Lynn's sixth-grade teacher, Dave Alberts, was a man who had attended medical school before becoming a teacher.

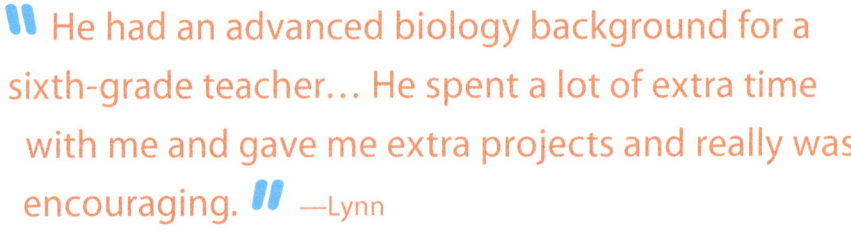

❝ He had an advanced biology background for a sixth-grade teacher… He spent a lot of extra time with me and gave me extra projects and really was encouraging. ❞ —Lynn

When Lynn went to Indiana University to obtain her Ph.D. degree, she was mentored by Tracy Sonneborn.

Sonneborn was the founder of the field of *protozoan genetics,* the study of inheritance in tiny living things called protozoa. He was also dedicated to teaching and mentoring.

❝ He was someone who was shortlisted for the Nobel Prize multiple times. ❞ —Lynn

Mycelium composite materials

A mushroom might be the most visible part of a fungus, but it is not the only part. The real work of decomposition and nutrient absorption is done in the thousands of threadlike cells within the soil or other *medium* (substance in which they are growing). These tiny, branching cells sometimes form a tangled mass called the *mycelium*.

In nature, a fungus's mycelium can bind with other mycelia and the growth medium to form thick mats. Scientists and **engineers** have modified the medium and other growing conditions in laboratory settings to coax the mycelia to bind together into a variety shapes. The result is a class of fungus-based materials called **mycelium composites.**

Mycelium composite bricks produced using yard waste and wood chips as growing media. Similar materials could be used to build habitats on the moon or Mars.

Down to Earth:

Ideas from space that could serve us on our planet.

Mycelium composites are catching on as building materials. Such waste materials as sawdust or yard clippings can be used as the growing medium. A mycelium composite's material properties—such as how strong or heavy it is—depend on the strains of fungi, the growing medium, and the conditions in which it was grown. So, there are endless possibilities! Designers are beginning to make bricks, furniture, tiles, and other products out of the material.

" There were people who were starting to build things with these filamentous fungi, using them to bind wood chips or garden clippings. " —Lynn

Fresh mycelium composite is firm but spongy, with a texture similar to that of polystyrene packing foam. Companies have already started using mycelium composites as a packaging material. They do not require oil or other fossil fuels to produce. They are also biodegradable and nontoxic.

This wine shipping container is made of mycelium composite grown from agricultural waste.

Big idea:
Inflatable-form mycotecture

Architects have envisioned large portions of buildings being made of mycelium composite materials. This idea is called *mycotecture*. *Mycotecture* is a combination of the root word *myco-*, meaning *fungi*, and *architecture*.

It would not be practical to make buildings out of mycelium composite bricks on the moon or Mars. The bricks would grow slowly, and then a **rover** would have to place them one-by-one—possibly with some sort of mortar between. Thousands of bricks would be needed to make a modest structure.

Instead, Lynn proposes that the fungal spores be loaded into an inflatable form, like a giant balloon. When the mission lands, the form would inflate to its full size. Mycelia would grow in it to strengthen it. This technique will allow the entire form to take shape at once, rather than being built up one or two bricks at a time.

Bio-bricks

Mycelium composite bricks may be too clunky for building an entire space colony. But, there is ongoing research and development on using such bricks for structures here on Earth. They may also serve as a complementary building material in off-planet structures. Team member Monika Lipińska has developed interlocking mycelium bricks that could be used to create foundations, outbuildings, or other structures.

Inventor feature: Hobbies and field trips

❝ I have an ever-expanding number of hobbies! ❞ —Lynn

Lynn plays many musical instruments, including the bagpipes. She began playing the bagpipes with her then-young son, who is now a world-class player.

❝ I learned to read music before I could read. ❞ —Lynn

Lynn also has many hobbies that include an element of microbial action. Baking, for example, often uses a single-celled fungus called yeast to make bread rise. Lynn also makes cheese. In cheesemaking, certain bacteria work to convert the liquid milk to solid cheese—with the help of the cheesemaker. Sometimes, even fungi are purposely introduced to the cheese to give it a distinctive flavor. Blue cheese is one such cheese.

Lynn and her children doing fieldwork at Yellowstone National Park, *top*. Lynn with her son, Kyle Rothschild, at the World Pipe Band Championships in Scotland, *right*.

> I love new things, I love hobbies, and I'm also curious how things are made. —Lynn

Lynn enjoys field trips to study **microbes**—and bringing her family with her. She took both of her children on their first field trip before they were a month old. They also made trips as toddlers to Yellowstone National Park, where Lynn and her husband were studying *extremophiles*. An extremophile is a living thing that grows best in environments that cannot easily support other life—for example, the hot springs of Yellowstone. Both children went on to become biologists.

Feeding the fungi

Unlike plants and other living things, fungi do not use **photosynthesis** to make their own food. They need to consume other organic material to grow. Lynn's team sees two options for feeding the fungi. First, the mycelia could grow in a concentrated nutrient solution. The solution could be pre-loaded into the form or delivered later and added to the form by robotic **rovers.**

A second option involves the use of the local **regolith,** another example of *in situ* resource utilization. Regolith is a powdery, rocky substance. **Microbes** that could *metabolize* (break down) regolith would be loaded into the form. When the mission arrived at the world, the form would inflate with **carbon dioxide.** At the same time, a construction rover would excavate regolith and deposit it into the form. The microbes would use the regolith, carbon dioxide, and added water to multiply, giving off oxygen as a waste product. In turn, the fungi would feed on these microbes and use the oxygen they produced to grow.

Lynn and her team are working on finding the ideal feeder microbe with which to load the form. The leading candidates are cyanobacteria and algae. Both are photosynthetic microbes.

Whatever the case, the fungi will need water to grow. Robotic **probes** will harvest nearby ice and deliver the water to the growing form.

Artist's impression of a rover delivering nutrient solution to an inflatable form on Mars

Cyanobacteria and algae are living things that make up pond scum.

Freshly grown mycelium composite materials are a bit soft to the touch, like freshly baked bread. That's an advantage in packing material but a disadvantage when greater strength is needed. Structures on the moon and Mars will have to withstand **micrometeoroid** impacts. Micrometeoroids are tiny, pebble-sized rocks that hurtle through space. They burn up in Earth's **atmosphere.** But, on bodies with little or no atmosphere—such as the moon and Mars—they crash into the surface and grind it into **regolith.**

A micrometeoroid would likely puncture a soft mycelium composite. But, the composite is strengthened when it is heated to a high temperature, much like a brick or clay pot in a kiln.

❝ When you bake the material, you end up with something like particle board. It becomes very hard and stiff. ❞ —Lynn

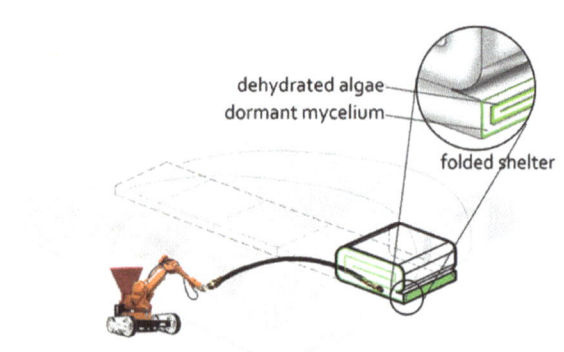

1

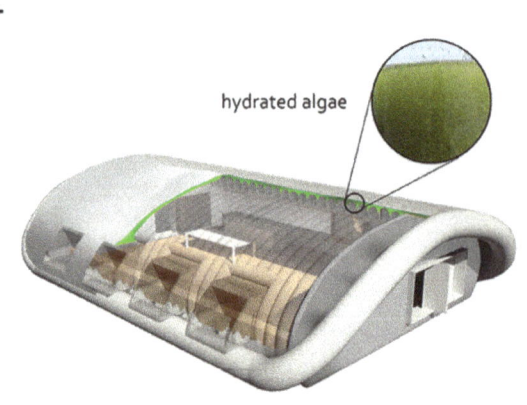

4

On Earth, the atmosphere helps distribute the sun's heat around the planet, limiting temperature extremes. On the moon, the lack of an atmosphere results in extreme temperature swings. During the lunar day, the sun bakes the surface to a temperature of 260 °F (127 °C)—hot enough to harden the exterior. On frigid Mars, baking the composite might require some other heating method.

Although the exterior of the form will be hardened, the interior may be left "soft" and alive. Maintaining a living interior surface will enable the form to repair itself. If a micrometeoroid hit the form, for example, crew members could fill the hole with a nutrient solution. The mycelium would regrow in the damaged area.

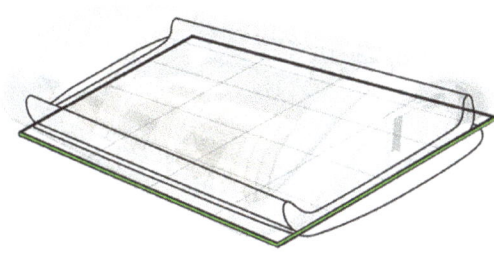

2

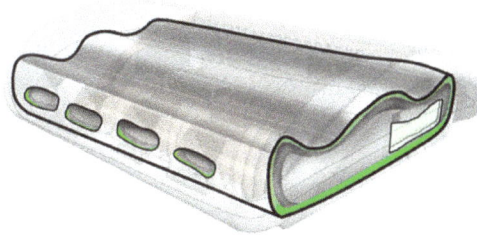

3

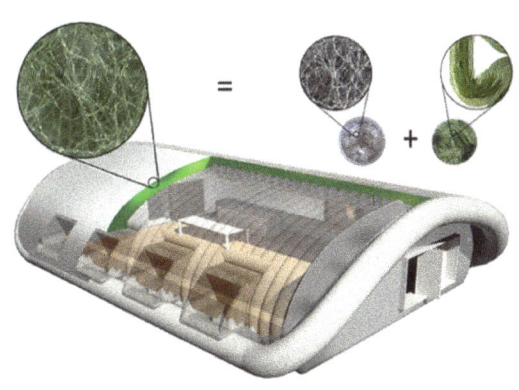

5

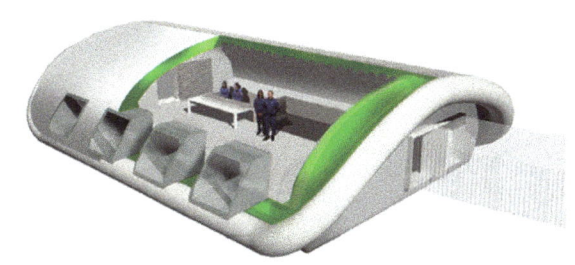

6

Prototypes

Lynn worked with a company called Moonprint Solutions to create a small-scale inflatable **prototype.** The team used a technique called *drop stitch* in the inflatable design. Drop-stitched materials have many long strands that run from one side of the form to the other. The strands hold the two sides together, while still allowing the interior to be filled with gas. Inflatable designs of all shapes and sizes can be created with drop stitch. Drop stitch is used on Earth to make things like paddle boards. In the form, the drop stitches will also serve as anchor points for the fungal mycelia.

Lynn's students have made stools out of baked mycelia to prove the technique works and to study growing media. These stools are lightweight, strong, and durable.

Lynn and her team examine a mycelium composite stool produced in their lab.

Down to Earth:

Ideas from space that could serve us on our planet.

Lynn is researching mycotecture technology with Chris Maurer, chief architect at Redhouse Studios. The studio is developing a promising use for the technology on Earth. The southwestern African country of Namibia suffers from drought, homelessness, and unemployment. A project called BioHAB is tackling all three problems. Workers will harvest blackthorn bushes, which absorb much water and choke out pastureland. The harvested blackthorn branches will be used to grow mushrooms, which can be eaten or sold. Workers will then convert the mycelium from the harvested mushrooms into bricks, which will be used to make houses and other structures in the area.

Inventor feature: Darwin

Lynn is a great admirer of the British scientist Charles Darwin. In the 1800's Darwin proposed the theory that all living things evolved (developed gradually) from a common ancestor through *natural selection*. Natural selection is a process in nature by which the living things best suited to their environment are the ones most likely to leave offspring.

> There were days that he thought that he could see what no one else could see, and there were days that he had a lot of self-doubt. —Lynn

Darwin was ahead of his time in many ways. He suffered from chronic illnesses, so he worked in a home laboratory and helped raise his children. His writings reveal the patience and warmth characteristic of his personality:

Charles Darwin with his oldest son, William Erasmus, in 1842

❝ He came in and one of his boys was bouncing on the sofa. In that Victorian era, the father would have had his head off or called in the mother to do it. He instead said, 'You had better get off the sofa, I told you I didn't want to see you jumping on it.' And the kid said to him, 'Well then I advise you to leave the room, Papa.' And he thought that was so cute, he wrote that down! ❞ —Lynn

Planetary protection

The environment of Mars is extreme. But, life on Earth has been finding ways to survive for billions of years. There's a possibility that some Earth life could hitchhike to the surface aboard **landers** and contaminate the Martian surface. So, when we look for life, we might find an unexpected visitor!

NASA has been aware of this possibility for decades. The agency puts each lander going to a place that could be habitable, such as Mars, through a thorough sterilization procedure. This procedure ensures that the landers are free of any **microbes** that could contaminate their destinations.

Orbiting probes, however, are not sterilized. Therefore, mission planners intentionally crash them into bodies that cannot sustain life to keep them from contaminating potentially life-harboring ones. For example, the Cassini probe crashed into Saturn at the end of its mission so it didn't careen into Titan or Enceladus later.

Lynn's inflatable structure, on the other hand, *must* contain living things. But, fungi are relatively delicate, so they do not represent a serious threat to colonize the surface of other worlds.

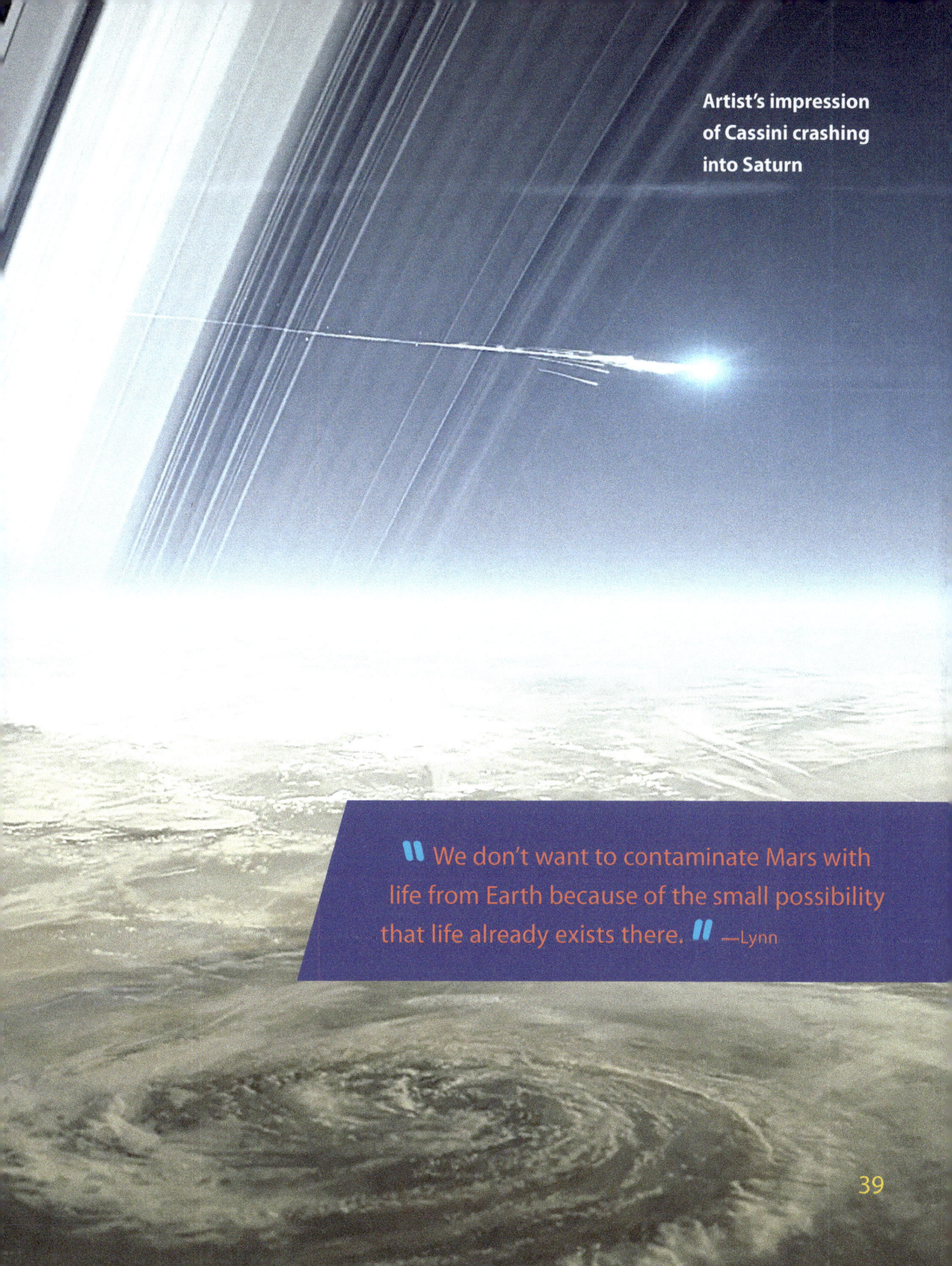

Artist's impression of Cassini crashing into Saturn

❚❚ We don't want to contaminate Mars with life from Earth because of the small possibility that life already exists there. ❚❚ —Lynn

> **Filamentous fungi in general are not particularly good at living at really high temperatures or really low temperatures and being active.** —Lynn

Feeder microbes might pose a higher risk. They must be hardy enough to grow in a wide range of conditions but still vulnerable to Mars's environment, so that they perish if they escape. Fortunately, the climate extremes and harmful **radiation** are likely to be enough to destroy any microbes that escape the inflated form.

Another option is to **engineer microbes** with special kill-switches in their genetic material. Such genetic sequences will cause the microbe to self-destruct under certain triggering conditions.

Down to Earth:

Ideas from space that could serve us on our planet.

Genetic kill-switches are an important part of safely using life as a technology. For example, other researchers are developing bacteria that can eat plastic waste. Plastic waste is a huge problem, but plastic is a major part of our lives. If plastic-eating bacteria escaped into the wild, they could wreak havoc on human civilization. Therefore, the researchers are incorporating strong kill-switches into these bacteria. These bacteria would only work in controlled environments, and they would destroy themselves if they moved out into the open.

The extreme conditions of Mars will keep any escaped microbes from colonizing the planet's surface.

Experiments

Of course, mycelium composites must undergo rigorous testing before mission planners will trust them to house and protect astronauts. Lynn's team is hard at work testing different composite samples to find one best suited to the many roles it will need to fulfill.

A group led by Debbie Senesky at Stanford University is testing the physical properties of various baked mycelium composites. So far, one sample has shown a compressive strength of 30 megapascals. That's stronger than concrete! Future experiments will test the composite's tensile strength. Tensile strength measures how much a substance can be pulled before it fails.

Samples were also tested in the Materials International Space Station Experiments (MISSE) over the course of about 160 days. MISSE samples are mounted on a panel outside the ISS and exposed to the harsh conditions of space. The experiments showed that the melanin present in the mycelia provided good **radiation** protection. Melanin is the same pigment present in people that colors our hair and skin.

Lynn's team has also enlisted the help of Michael Rheinstadter at McMaster University in Ontario, Canada. The university's Planetary Simulator is subjecting mycelium samples to many of the variables seen on the moon and Mars, including extremes of temperature, pressure, gas concentration, and radiation.

MISSE samples (the small squares below) sit exposed to the conditions of space aboard the ISS.

Lynn's team

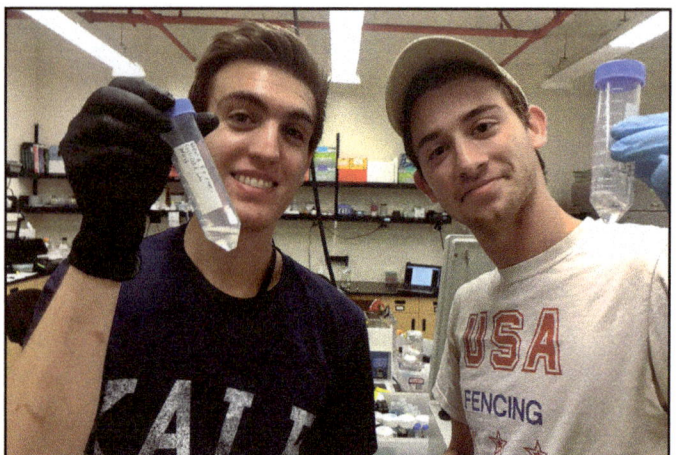

Students in Lynn Rothschild's lab at NASA Ames Research Center in Mountain View, California, are involved in research into mycelium composites and related fields.

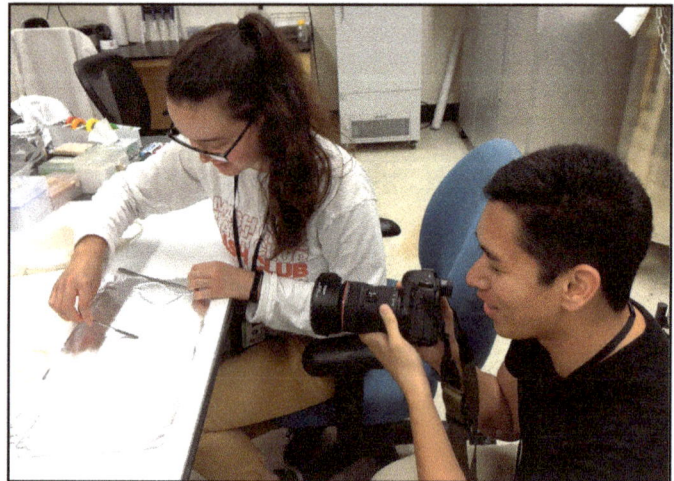

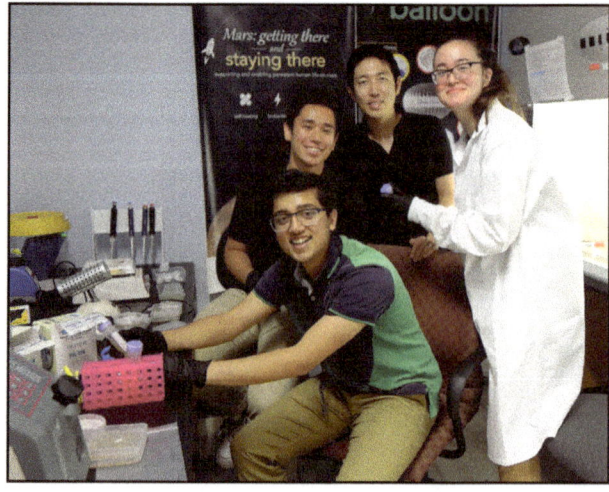

Glossary

astrobiology the search for and study of life in the universe.

atmosphere the mass of gases that surrounds a planet.

carbon dioxide a colorless, odorless gas present in the atmospheres of many planets, including Earth.

ecosystem a system made up of living things and their environment, or the place they live. The living things in an ecosystem depend on one another and on their environment to provide the things that they need, such as food and shelter.

engineer a person who uses scientific principles to design structures, such as bridges and skyscrapers, machines, and all sorts of products.

habitat living area.

lander a spacecraft designed to land on a planet, moon, or other body in space.

microbe a very small living thing.

micrometeoroid an object less than 0.04 inch (1 millimeter) wide floating in space.

orbit a looping path around an object in space; the condition of circling a massive object in space under the influence of the object's gravity.

photosynthesis the process by which plants and other living things make food from carbon dioxide and water.

probe a rocket, satellite, or other uncrewed spacecraft carrying scientific instruments, to record or report back information about space.

prototype a functional experimental model of an invention.

radiation energy given off in the form of waves or tiny particles of matter.

regolith loose rock fragments, from large boulders to dust, covering solid rock.

rover a lander designed to move about for surface exploration.

Review and reflect

Now that you've finished reading about Lynn Rothschild, use these pages to think about her experiences and mycotecture habitats in new ways. As you work, reflect on the importance of creative problem solving, curiosity, and open-mindedness in life.

Complex problems and creative solutions

Why are scientists interested in establishing permanent bases on the moon and Mars?

What are some of the problems associated with establishing permanent bases on the moon and Mars?

How does Lynn Rothschild hope to overcome these challenges with mycotecture habitats? What makes this solution so innovative?

Visit www.worldbook.com/resources to download sample answers, blank graphic organizers, and a rubric to evaluate writing.

Inspiration can come from anywhere!

Use a graphic organizer like the one below to map out your ideas. What ideas or experiences led to Lynn's innovative solution?

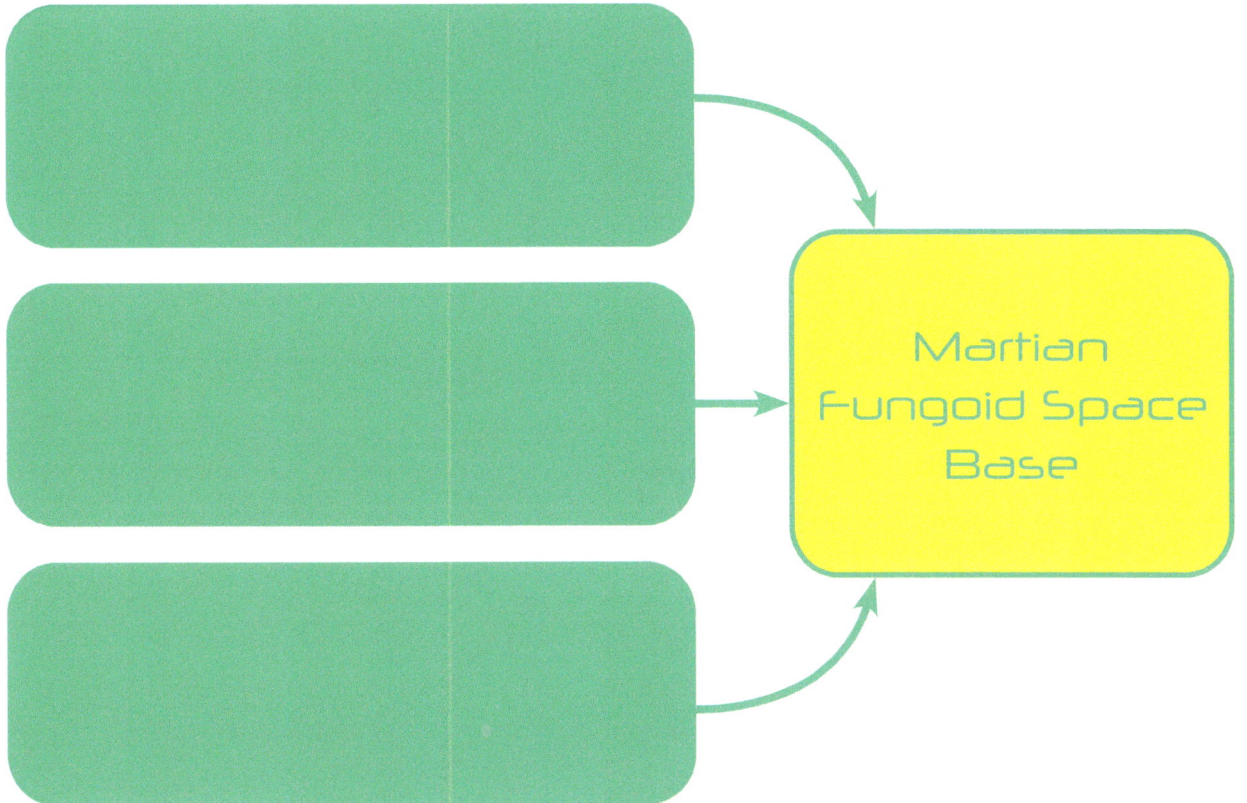

Write about it!

Think about Lynn's experiences in life and as a NIAC Fellow.

How have Lynn and her team used unconventional techniques to develop new methods for building habitats on the moon and Mars? Why might it be important to think outside the box when looking for innovative solutions?

Index

A

algae, 30-31
amebas, 10-11
Ames Research Center, 4
antibiotics, 20
Armillaria ostoyae, 21
astrobiology, 11, 14
astronauts, 4-8, 12-13, 17, 42
atmosphere, 4, 32-33

B

bacteria, 20, 28, 30-31, 41
biological waste, 24-25
birds, 8-9
bricks, mycelium composite, 24-25, 27, 35

C

carbon dioxide, 30
Cassini probe, 38
colonization of space, 4, 8, 16, 27
compressive strength, 42
cyanobacteria, 30-31

D

Darwin, Charles, 36-37
decomposition, 19, 21, 24
drop stitch, 34

E

Enceladus, 38
extremophiles, 29

F

feeder microbes, 30, 40
filamentous fungi, 25, 40
fungi, definition of, 18-19

G

genetic kill-switches, 40-41

H

habitats, 6, 24
Hubble Space Telescope, 11

I

ice. *See* water ice
in situ resource utilization (ISRU), 13, 30
infections, 20
International Space Station (ISS), 42

M

Mars, missions to, 6-8, 12-13, 27
Materials International Space Station Experiments (MISSE), 42
McMaster University, 43
medical care, 8, 17
melanin, 42
microbes, 5, 10, 17, 28-31, 38, 40. *See also* bacteria
micrometeoroids, 32-33
microscopes, 10-11
molds, 20
moon, missions to, 12-13, 27
mushrooms, 19-20, 35
mycelium, definition of, 24
mycelium composites, 24-27, 32-35, 42-43
mycotecture, 26-27, 32-35

N

National Aeronautics and Space Administration (NASA), 4-5, 14, 38
natural selection, 36
nutrients, 19, 21, 24, 30, 33

O

orbits, 7, 38
oxygen, 4, 13, 30

P

penicillin, 20
plastic waste, 41
probes, 6, 30, 38
protozoa, 10-11, 23

R

radiation, 4, 40, 42-43
regolith, 30, 32
rhizomorphs, 21
robotic technology, 6, 13, 30
rovers, 27, 30

S

Saturn, 38-39
spacecraft, 6
spores, 19-20, 27
Stanford University, 11, 42
sterilization, 38
sun, 30, 33
supplies for space missions, 6, 12

T

tensile strength, 42
temperature, 4, 32-33, 40, 43
tensile strength, 42
Titan, 38
trees, 21
turtles, 6

W

water ice, 13, 30

Y

yeast, 28
Yellowstone National Park, 29